Helping People See

Monika Davies

✳ Smithsonian

Contributing Author

Allison Duarte, M.A.

Consultants

Tamieka Grizzle, Ed.D.
K–5 STEM Lab Instructor
Harmony Leland Elementary School

Brian Mandell, Ph.D.
Div. Dir. of Curriculum & Communications
Smithsonian

Publishing Credits

Rachelle Cracchiolo, M.S.Ed., *Publisher*
Conni Medina, M.A.Ed., *Managing Editor*
Diana Kenney, M.A.Ed., NBCT, *Content Director*
Véronique Bos, *Creative Director*
June Kikuchi, *Content Director*
Robin Erickson, *Art Director*
Seth Rogers, *Editor*
Mindy Duits, *Senior Graphic Designer*
Smithsonian Science Education Center

Image Credits: front cover, p.1 Paolo Bona/Shutterstock; p.4 (insert) Martyn F. Chillmaid/Science Source; p.10 Bellena/Shutterstock; p.11 (all except 2nd from bottom), p.21 (left), 32 (left) ⊠ Smithsonian; p.12 (illustration) Timothy J. Bradley; p.13 Dan Hixson/University of Utah College of Engineering; p.16 Solent News/Splash News/Newscom; p.17 (top) Jeremias Costilla/iStock; p.17 (bottom) Ferrantraite/iStock; p.20 Rex Features via AP Images; p.21 (right) Cecilia/Creative Commons 2.0; p.22 (bottom) Eric Cohen/Science Source ; p.23 (bottom) Babak Tafreshi/Science Source; p.25 Courtesy of Peter Erskine; p.27 (top) Ute Grabowsky/photothek images UG/Alamy; all other images iStock and/or Shutterstock.

Library of Congress Cataloging-in-Publication Data

Names: Davies, Monika, author.
Title: Helping people see / Monika Davies.
Description: Huntington Beach, CA : Teacher Created Materials, [2018] | Audience: K to grade 3. | Includes index. |
Identifiers: LCCN 2017060492 (print) | LCCN 2017061412 (ebook) | ISBN 9781493869268 (e-book) | ISBN 9781493866861 (pbk.)
Subjects: LCSH: Optical instruments--Juvenile literature. | Optics--Technological innovations--Juvenile literature.
Classification: LCC QC371.4 (ebook) | LCC QC371.4 .D38 2018 (print) | DDC 535--dc23
LC record available at https://lccn.loc.gov/2017060492

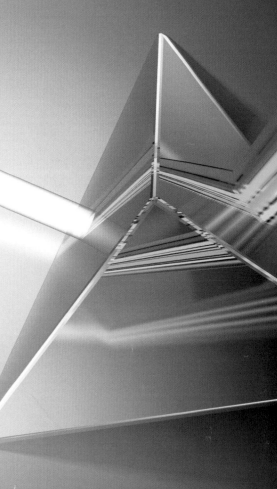

☀ Smithsonian

Teacher Created Materials

5301 Oceanus Drive
Huntington Beach, CA 92649-1030
www.tcmpub.com

ISBN 978-1-4938-6686-1
© 2019 Teacher Created Materials, Inc.
Printed in China
Nordica.042018.CA21800320

Table of Contents

Seeing the Light

Our eyes let us see the world. Yet human eyes are far from perfect. Only some people have 20/20, or normal, vision. And it's tough for our eyes to catch tiny details, such as stars way up in the night sky.

Over the years, people have tried to improve sight. This has led to the world of optics. Optics is the study of light and how it travels. Light is the key to sight. When we see an object, we see light bouncing off that object.

Light bounces off of a mirror.

What are some innovations that have changed how we see the world? Glasses, goggles, and prisms are just a few. Dive into the world of optics, where light bounces and bends so people can see!

Soap bubbles reflect many different colors.

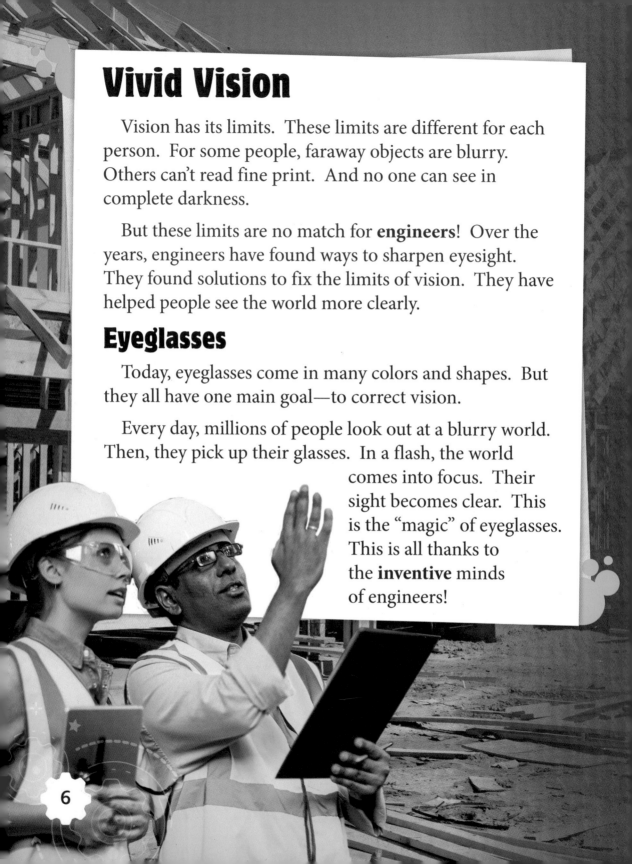

Vivid Vision

Vision has its limits. These limits are different for each person. For some people, faraway objects are blurry. Others can't read fine print. And no one can see in complete darkness.

But these limits are no match for **engineers**! Over the years, engineers have found ways to sharpen eyesight. They found solutions to fix the limits of vision. They have helped people see the world more clearly.

Eyeglasses

Today, eyeglasses come in many colors and shapes. But they all have one main goal—to correct vision.

Every day, millions of people look out at a blurry world. Then, they pick up their glasses. In a flash, the world comes into focus. Their sight becomes clear. This is the "magic" of eyeglasses. This is all thanks to the **inventive** minds of engineers!

A girl gets new glasses.

Nero (NEE-roh), a Roman Emperor, may have used the first "lens." Some people say he held an emerald to his eye at the gladiator games to help him see the games from far away.

Some inventions start with small discoveries. For example, when a jar of water was placed on a sheet of paper, something interesting happened to the text. The water made the words look bigger! People wondered why this was the case. They began researching. Soon, they found that crystals could do the same thing. This led to the first magnifying glass and then to glasses.

The first glasses were simple. People held them up to their faces. The lenses were very heavy. But they worked!

No one knows who invented glasses. But, in Europe, **monks** were the first to wear them. In the late thirteenth century, Italian monks read texts for hours at a time. As they aged, their eyesight got worse. Words began to blur. The monks needed something to help them see the words clearly. Glasses helped correct their vision.

Water magnifies text and other objects.

calcite crystal

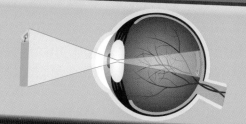

Normal Vision
Light focuses on the back of the eye.

Nearsighted

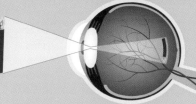

Light focuses in front of the back of the eye.

lens →

Vision is corrected with a lens.

Farsighted

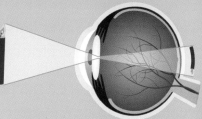

Light focuses behind the back of the eye.

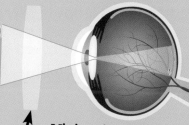

lens →

Vision is corrected with a lens.

SCIENCE

Spectacle Science

If you are nearsighted (unable to clearly see things far away) or farsighted (unable to clearly see things up close), light is not focusing on the back of the eye. To correct this, different lenses are used. The lenses bend the light so that it focuses where it should.

Hundreds of years later, the printing press was invented. Books could be made in large quantities. Soon, more people were reading. This meant more people needed glasses.

Some people had to wear glasses all day. At first, engineers made nose **bridges** to hold the lenses together. These bridges sat on people's noses. But the glasses fell off a lot. In time, frames with arms that curled around the ears were added. **Quartz** lenses were swapped out for glass. Then, plastic lenses took the place of glass.

Now, glasses are a part of many people's lives. We can wear them all day, every day. There are many types of lenses to sharpen our vision. If you have trouble seeing things at a distance, there are glasses for you. If you have to squint to read a book, there's a pair of lenses that can help.

Glasses have improved many lives. For many people, the world is no longer a blur. With glasses, the world can come into focus.

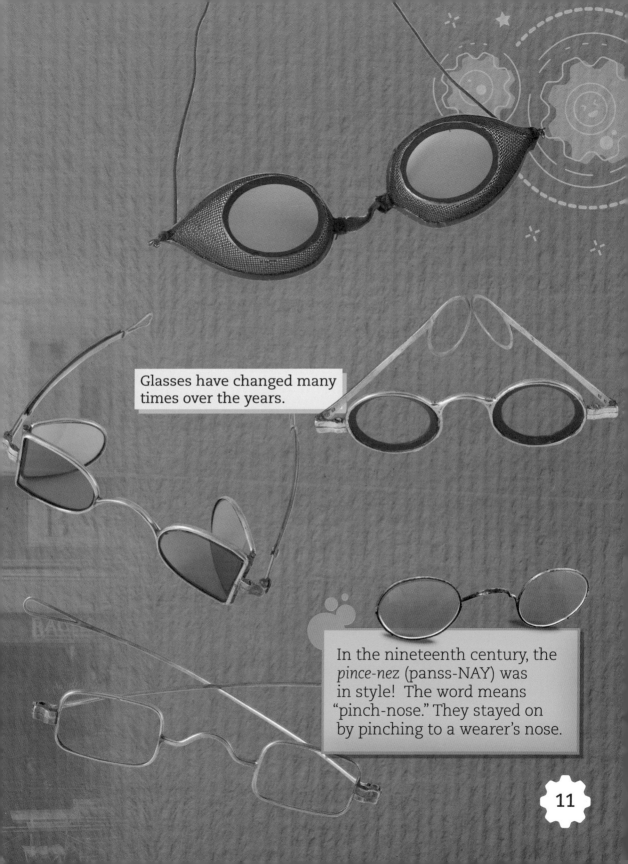

Glasses have changed many times over the years.

In the nineteenth century, the *pince-nez* (panss-NAY) was in style! The word means "pinch-nose." They stayed on by pinching to a wearer's nose.

11

Liquid-Based Lenses

The search for the perfect lens is still going. Engineers are always looking for new ways to make better lenses. In Utah, they are using something new to make lenses—liquid! These lenses are adaptive. They can figure out what you are looking at. Then, they adjust on their own so your eyes can focus on the right place.

How do they work? There is a distance meter in the bridge of the glasses. It measures how far an object is from your eyes. The lenses in the glasses are made out of glycerin (GLIH-suh-rin), a thick, clear liquid. It is kept inside a thin membrane that can move. When the meter detects how far an object is from you, it adjusts the lenses. This changes the curve of the lens. Then, when light passes through them, it hits your eye in the right spot. With these glasses, you can see any object clearly— near or far.

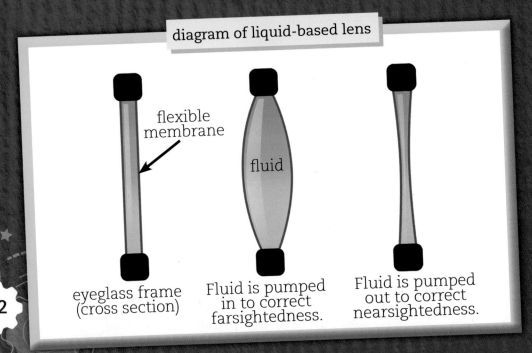

diagram of liquid-based lens

flexible membrane

fluid

eyeglass frame (cross section)

Fluid is pumped in to correct farsightedness.

Fluid is pumped out to correct nearsightedness.

Adaptive lenses will be controlled with a smartphone. When your eyewear **prescription** changes, you add the new numbers to the app. Your lenses will then adjust.

The creators of liquid-based lenses look at their work.

Color-Correcting Glasses

Glasses can also help color-blind people see colors. About 1 in 10 people in the United States has color blindness. Some people can't see any color at all. They see the world in shades of gray. For others, color pairs, such as red and green or blue and yellow, look brown or black.

Enchroma (en-KROH-muh) is a company that wants to help. It makes glasses with special lenses. Each lens has a **filter**. The filters make some colors easier to see.

Night-Vision Goggles

Eyes need light to see. Night-vision goggles help people see in the dark. Our eyes can see **visible light**. But we can't see **infrared light**. This kind of light is felt as heat. People's bodies give off heat. Night-vision goggles help us "see" body heat. They do this by turning infrared light into visible light. No one can hide in the dark with these goggles out there!

Night-vision goggles are used by many soldiers. They help soldiers see in the dark and catch anyone trying to sneak up on them.

average color-blind view

normal vision using
Enchroma glasses

severe color-blind view

"Smart" Glasses

Some people are adding technology to glasses. These new "smart" glasses can do much more than just fix your vision. They are also a fun way to view the world.

Snap's Spectacles are a stylish way to take pictures. Each pair comes with a small camera in the frame. The wearer pushes a button. This "snaps" a 10-second video. The video is then saved online.

Vue glasses look like regular glasses. But they can do much more. You can use them to call home or play music. They can even remind you of items on your to-do list! All this technology is kept in thin, sleek frames.

Vue glasses

Snap's Spectacles with camera

TECHNOLOGY

Put to Work

Google™ has designed smart glasses for factory workers. They make work faster and easier. These glasses let workers see directions and videos that will help them do their jobs. This is a good way to keep workers' hands free to do other things.

Fine-Tuned Focus

Everywhere we look, there are things that are hard to see. They might be stars high in the sky. Or they might be cells that lie under our skin. These tiny details can't be seen without help. They can only be seen through special devices. These unique tools are known as optical equipment. Using these devices, we have learned a lot about our world and the universe.

Microscopes

Once, we could not see anything finer than a strand of hair. Cells were hidden from us. So we did not understand how the human body worked. But all of that changed with the invention of the microscope.

Microscopes let people see small things. They act like strong magnifying glasses. They use lenses and light to make objects look bigger. This lets us explore hidden details.

This student uses a microscope.

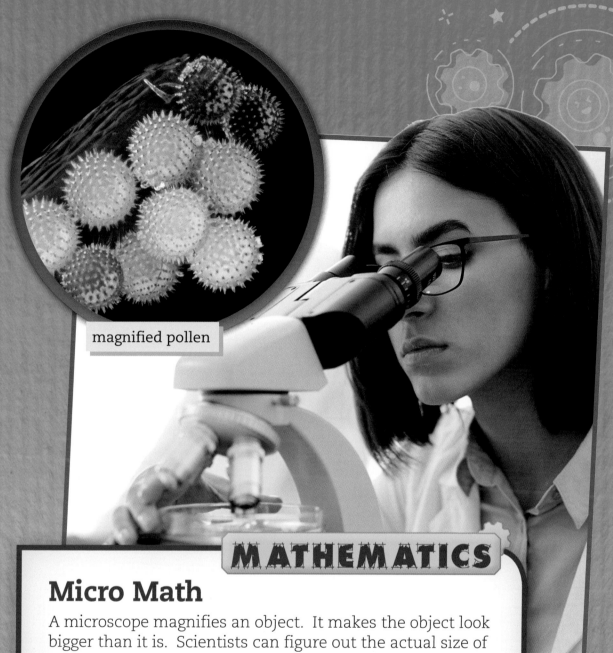

magnified pollen

Micro Math

A microscope magnifies an object. It makes the object look bigger than it is. Scientists can figure out the actual size of the object they are studying. To do this, they use division. First, they use a micro-ruler to measure what they see. Then, they divide the measurement by the magnification. Their answer is the actual size of the object.

object measurement ÷ magnification = actual size

In 1590, the first compound microscope was created. Three Dutch men came up with the idea. First, they took two lenses. One lens was placed at the bottom of a tube. The other was placed at the top. They then looked through the two lenses. Objects looked bigger through the lenses. The men could focus on details. Their first close-ups were blurry. But the idea started the development of microscopes.

Over time, the quality of lenses improved. Soon, microscopes could look inside cells. Big discoveries were made. For instance, scientists could study diseases. They could find harmful germs. These findings helped lead to cures.

Microscopes are used in other types of work. Doctors use them for surgeries. Jewelers use them to look at gems. People who study crime scenes use them to look at evidence. This tool has had an effect on the way we view the world in many ways.

This is a paper microscope called a Foldscope™.

1855–1860 classroom microscope

The first microscopes were made of wood and cardboard. They were also decorated with fish skin!

1750 Edmund Culpeper microscope

Telescopes

Telescopes let us see things that are far away. One of the first people to use a telescope was Galileo. He was a famous scientist. He built his first telescope in 1609. Galileo found many things with his telescope. He saw peaks on Earth's moon. He saw Jupiter's moons. He counted stars in the Milky Way. This is all thanks to his telescope!

There are two main types of telescopes. One is the **refracting** telescope. It has two lenses that make objects look larger than they really are. One big lens focuses light. A small lens projects the light into the eye. The lenses are set in long tubes. The bigger the lens, the farther away people can see. The second is the **reflecting** telescope. It bounces light off mirrors and into the eye.

Telescopes help us see what lies beyond Earth. They help us learn about the universe. To this day, we are still looking at the stars in the sky.

Galileo looks at the stars through his telescope.

reflecting telescope

Giant Magellan Telescope

Giant Telescope

Scientists are building a huge reflecting telescope, called the Giant Magellan Telescope, in Chile. It is more than $24\frac{1}{2}$ meters (80 feet) wide. It will use seven mirrors to look at outer space. The mirrors are set in a shape that looks like a honeycomb. It will be able to capture faint images from outer space.

Prisms

A prism is a solid piece of glass with flat sides. When white light shines into a prism, a rainbow of colors shines out. This can make for a stunning sight.

How does this happen? A prism refracts, or bends, light. All the colors that make up white light separate. Shorter wavelengths, such as violet, bend more than longer wavelengths, such as red. This makes the "solid" white light break into a rainbow of colors as it passes through the prism. The rainbow is called a spectrum.

Prisms are used in many things. You can find them in binoculars. They help bend light to make objects seem bigger. Some digital cameras use prisms to help make their colors more lifelike. Sometimes, prisms are even used to create art.

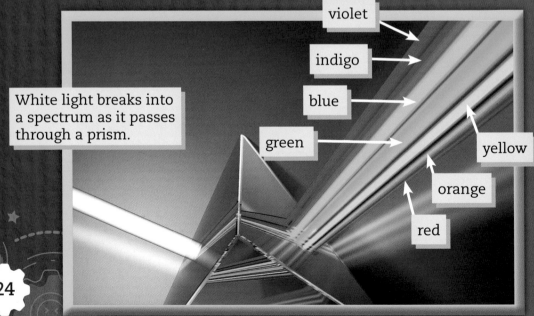

White light breaks into a spectrum as it passes through a prism.

violet

indigo

blue

green

yellow

orange

red

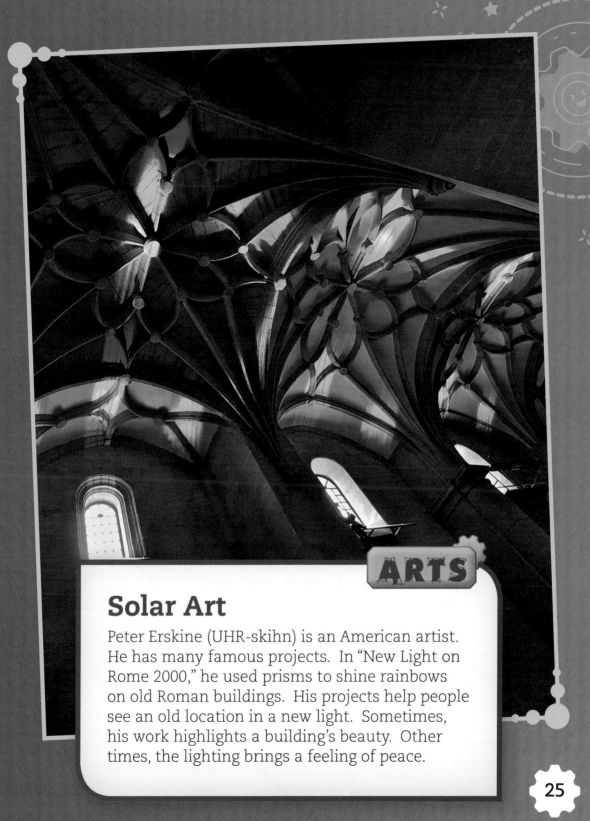

Solar Art

Peter Erskine (UHR-skihn) is an American artist. He has many famous projects. In "New Light on Rome 2000," he used prisms to shine rainbows on old Roman buildings. His projects help people see an old location in a new light. Sometimes, his work highlights a building's beauty. Other times, the lighting brings a feeling of peace.

A Clearer Future

The world of optics is packed with innovations. Engineers and scientists change how we see the world. They come up with new ways to bend light. They use mirrors and lenses to help us see more clearly. Their ideas expand our view of the world—and of space!

Smart engineering is the key. It is the reason we have sharp vision. It is also why we can see hidden details. And it's how we see the stars above.

But there is so much that we have yet to see and understand. We are still learning. We have not yet seen every galaxy. We keep making new glasses to fit our needs. And we will always need to examine the smallest parts of life.

Every day, engineers come up with new ideas. Their ideas power more discoveries. Inventive minds are why we will continue to "see" a brighter future.

A student and teacher work in an optical lab.

A woman puts on contact lenses.

27

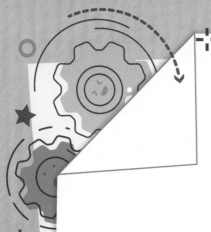

STEAM CHALLENGE

Define the Problem

A sporting company wants to make a new model of eyeglasses for triathlons. During a triathlon, athletes swim, run, and bike. It is important that the glasses are comfortable and stay in place. This way, athletes can focus on the race! The company has asked you to design and build a model.

 Constraints: You must use all flexible materials that can be stored in a small space.

 Criteria: A successful design will stay in place while the wearer runs in place for one minute.

Research and Brainstorm

Why do people use eyeglasses? In what ways have engineers changed the design of eyeglasses to serve special purposes? Why might an athlete need to use eyeglasses?

Design and Build

Sketch your glasses design. What purpose will each part serve? What materials will work best? Build the model.

Test and Improve

Wear the glasses. Then, run in place for one minute. Did the glasses stay in place? How can you improve them? Modify your design, and try again.

Reflect and Share

What other ways can you test the design? Will your design work in water? What can you add to make the glasses more attractive to athletes?

Glossary

adaptive—able to change

bridges—the parts of eyeglasses that rest on people's noses

engineers—people who design and build complex products, systems, machines, or structures

filter—a device that prevents things from passing through

infrared light—a type of light that cannot be seen by human eyes

innovations—new ideas, methods, or devices

inventive—having or showing an ability to think of new ideas and methods

membrane—a thin, soft, flexible layer

monks—men from certain religious communities who usually stay unmarried and live separate from society

prescription—an official note from a doctor that tells someone to use or do something

quartz—a naturally occurring substance that is usually found in the form of a hard, glossy crystal

reflecting—causing light, heat, or sound to move or bounce away in a different direction

refracting—causing light to bend as it passes through

spectrum—the colors that a ray of light can be split into

visible light—a type of light that can be seen by most human eyes

Index

Do you want to help people see better?
Here are some tips to get you started.

"When it comes to improving our vision, most people think of eyeglasses. But optics include all kinds of equipment that help us see things better. To work in this field, you must excel in science, math, and engineering in school. And always think outside the box—you might just come up with an idea for a new type of optics!" —**Brian Mandell, Ph.D., Division Director of Curriculum & Communications**

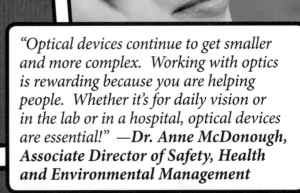

"Optical devices continue to get smaller and more complex. Working with optics is rewarding because you are helping people. Whether it's for daily vision or in the lab or in a hospital, optical devices are essential!" —**Dr. Anne McDonough, Associate Director of Safety, Health and Environmental Management**